T0389991

FIRST WORDS IN...
Italian

italiano

famiglia

palla

fratello

scarpa

by Christina Leaf

BELLWETHER MEDIA • MINNEAPOLIS, MN

BLASTOFF! READERS

Blastoff! Readers are carefully developed by literacy experts to build reading stamina and move students toward fluency by combining standards-based content with developmentally appropriate text.

 **Level 1** provides the most support through repetition of high-frequency words, light text, predictable sentence patterns, and strong visual support.

 **Level 2** offers early readers a bit more challenge through varied sentences, increased text load, and text-supportive special features.

 **Level 3** advances early-fluent readers toward fluency through increased text load, less reliance on photos, advancing concepts, longer sentences, and more complex special features.

★ **Blastoff! Universe**

Reading Level

  Grade **K**

  Grades **1–3**

 Grade **4**

This edition first published in 2026 by Bellwether Media, Inc.

No part of this publication may be reproduced in whole or in part without written permission of the publisher. For information regarding permission, write to Bellwether Media, Inc., Attention: Permissions Department, 3500 American Blvd W, Suite 150, Bloomington, MN 55431.

Library of Congress Cataloging-in-Publication Data

LC record for Italian available at: https://lccn.loc.gov/2025019030

Editor: Suzane Nguyen   Designer: Andrea Schneider

Printed in the United States of America, North Mankato, MN.

anana

Table of **Contents**

Buongiorno!

Buongiorno!

Mi chiamo Nico.

I live in Italy.

I speak *italiano*!

ciao (chow)
hello/goodbye

Words to Know

- buongiorno (bwon-JOR-noh).....................
....good morning
- mi chiamo (me key-AH-moh)......................
....my name is
- italiano (ee-tahl-ee-AH-noh) .... Italian
- per favore (per fah-VOHR-eh) ...... please
- grazie (GRAHT-zee-eh).............thank you

5

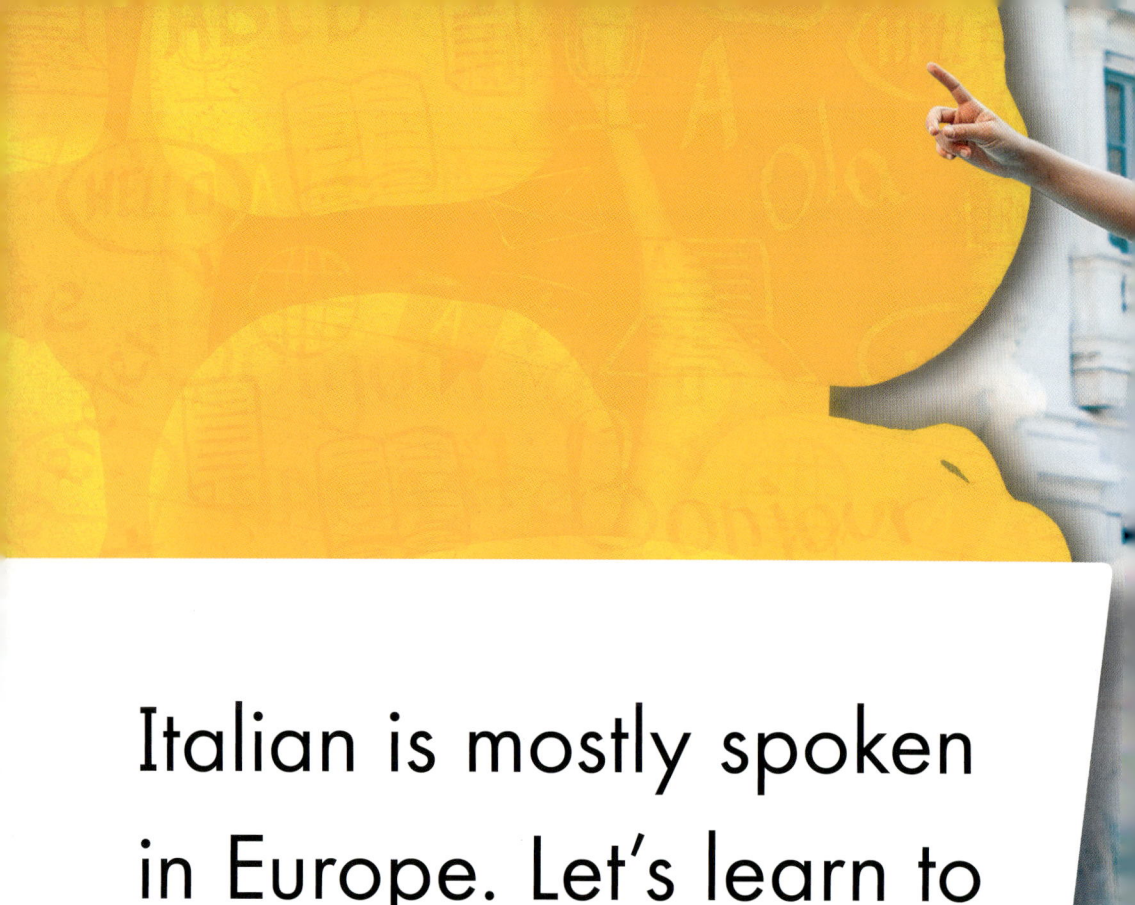

Italian is mostly spoken in Europe. Let's learn to speak Italian together!

Italian-speaking Countries

Europe

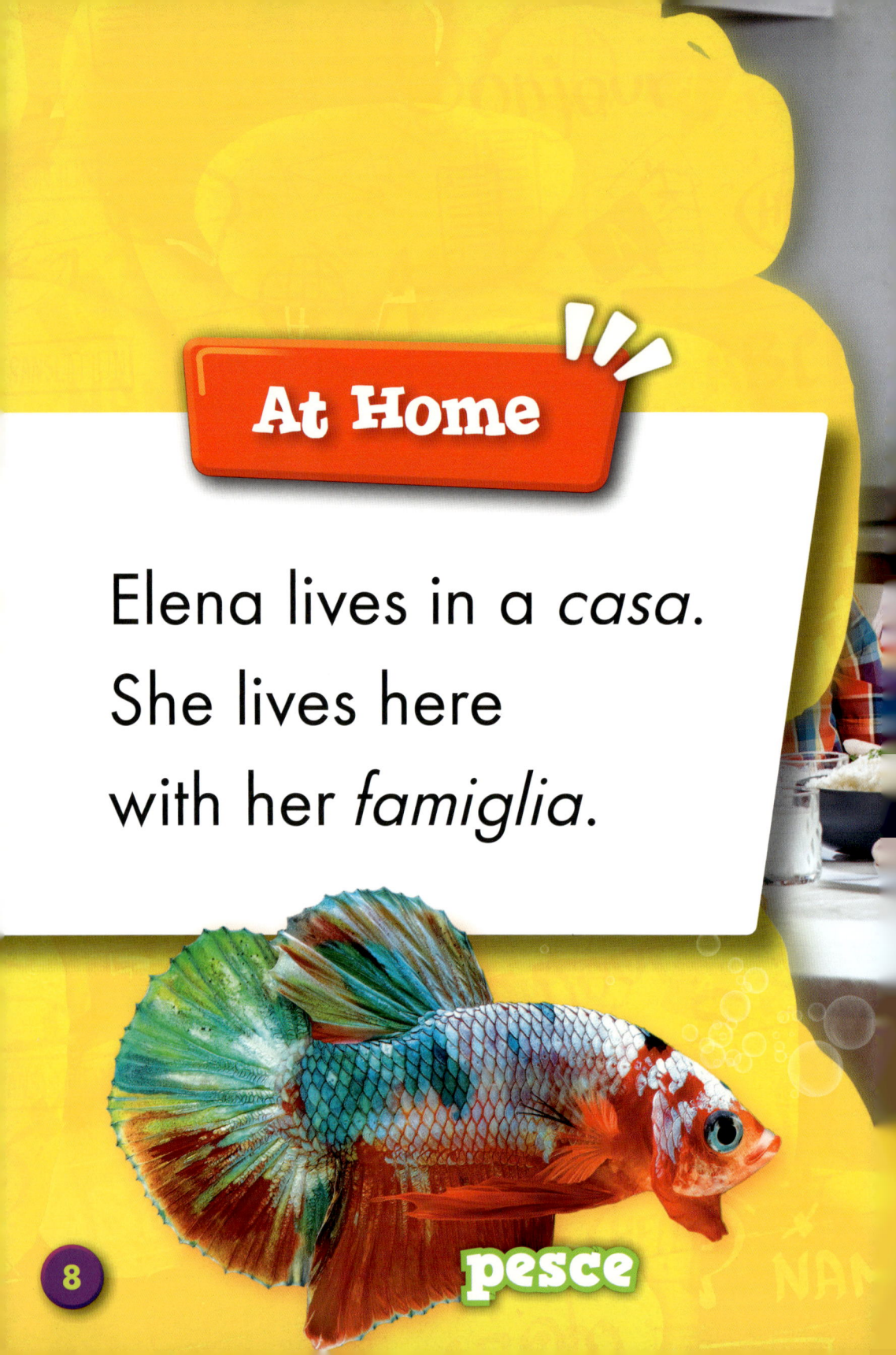

At Home

Elena lives in a *casa*.
She lives here
with her *famiglia*.

8

pesce

sorella

fratello

Words to Know

- famiglia (fah-MEEL-yah)..............family
- madre (MAH-dreh).........................mother
- padre (PAH-dreh)...........................father
- fratello (frah-TEL-loh)...............brother
- sorella (sohr-EL-lah)....................sister
- casa (CAH-zah) ....house
- cane (CAH-nay).................................dog
- pesce (PEH-sheh)...............................fish
- coniglio (coh-NEEL-yoh)...............rabbit

Leo eats *colazione* each *mattina*. Today he has *pane* with jam.

tazza

10

Words to Know

- colazione (coh-LAHT-ZEE-oh-neh)............ breakfast
- mattina (mah-TEE-nah)............. morning
- pane (PAH-neh) .... bread
- tazza (TAHT-zah) .... cup
- formaggio (for-MAH-joh) .... cheese
- anana (AH-nah-nah) .... pineapple

pane

Sofia walks to *scuola*. The art *insegnante* has paper and *forbici* ready!

forbici

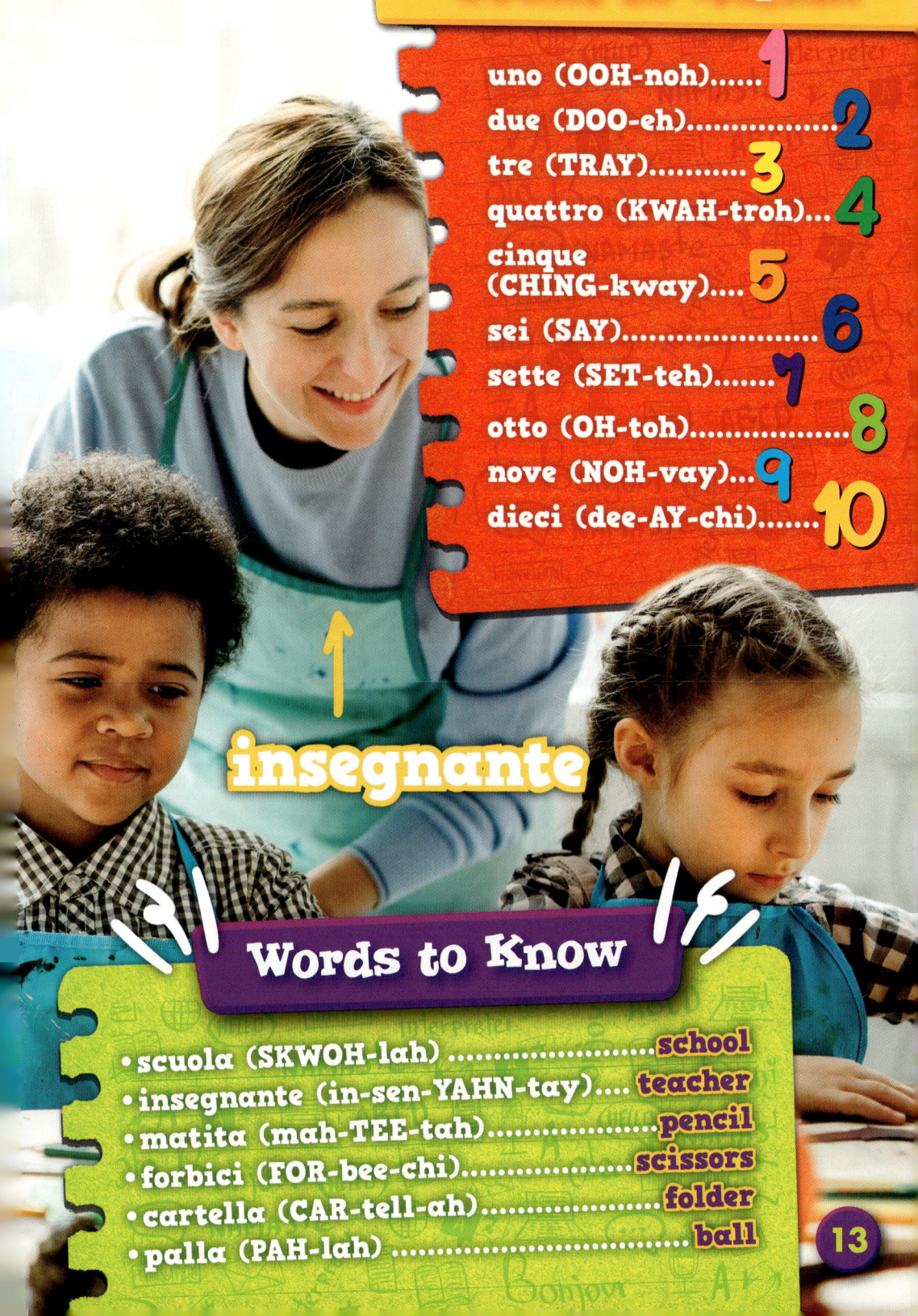

Count in Italian

uno (OOH-noh)......**1**
due (DOO-eh)..................**2**
tre (TRAY)...........**3**
quattro (KWAH-troh)...**4**
cinque (CHING-kway)....**5**
sei (SAY).....................**6**
sette (SET-teh).......**7**
otto (OH-toh)..................**8**
nove (NOH-vay)...**9**
dieci (dee-AY-chi).......**10**

insegnante

Words to Know

- scuola (SKWOH-lah) ....**school**
- insegnante (in-sen-YAHN-tay)....**teacher**
- matita (mah-TEE-tah).....................**pencil**
- forbici (FOR-bee-chi).....................**scissors**
- cartella (CAR-tell-ah)....................**folder**
- palla (PAH-lah) ....**ball**

13

Liam's *famiglia* takes a **passeggiata**. They talk with an *amico* at the **piazza**.

Words to Know

- **passeggiata** (pah-say-GEE-ah-tah) .... **evening walk**
- **scarpa** (SKAR-pah) .... **shoe**
- **piazza** (pee-AHT-zah) .... **town square**
- **amico** (ah-MEE-koh) .... **friend (male)**
- **amica** (ah-MEE-kah) ...... **friend (female)**

famiglia

Bianca eats **pasta al pomodoro** for *cena*. For *dolce*, she eats **gelato**.

gelato

verdure

bicchiere

Words to Know

- cena (CHE-nah).....................................**dinner**
- dolce (DOHL-chay)..............................**dessert**
- piatto (pee-AH-toh).............................**plate**
- forchetta (for-KAY-tah) ....**fork**
- cucchiaio (coo-KEE-EYE-oh)..............**spoon**
- bicchiere (bee-kee-ER-eh)..**drinking glass**
- verdure (ver-DUR-eh)..................**vegetables**
- pomodoro (poh-moh-DOR-oh)..........**tomato**

17

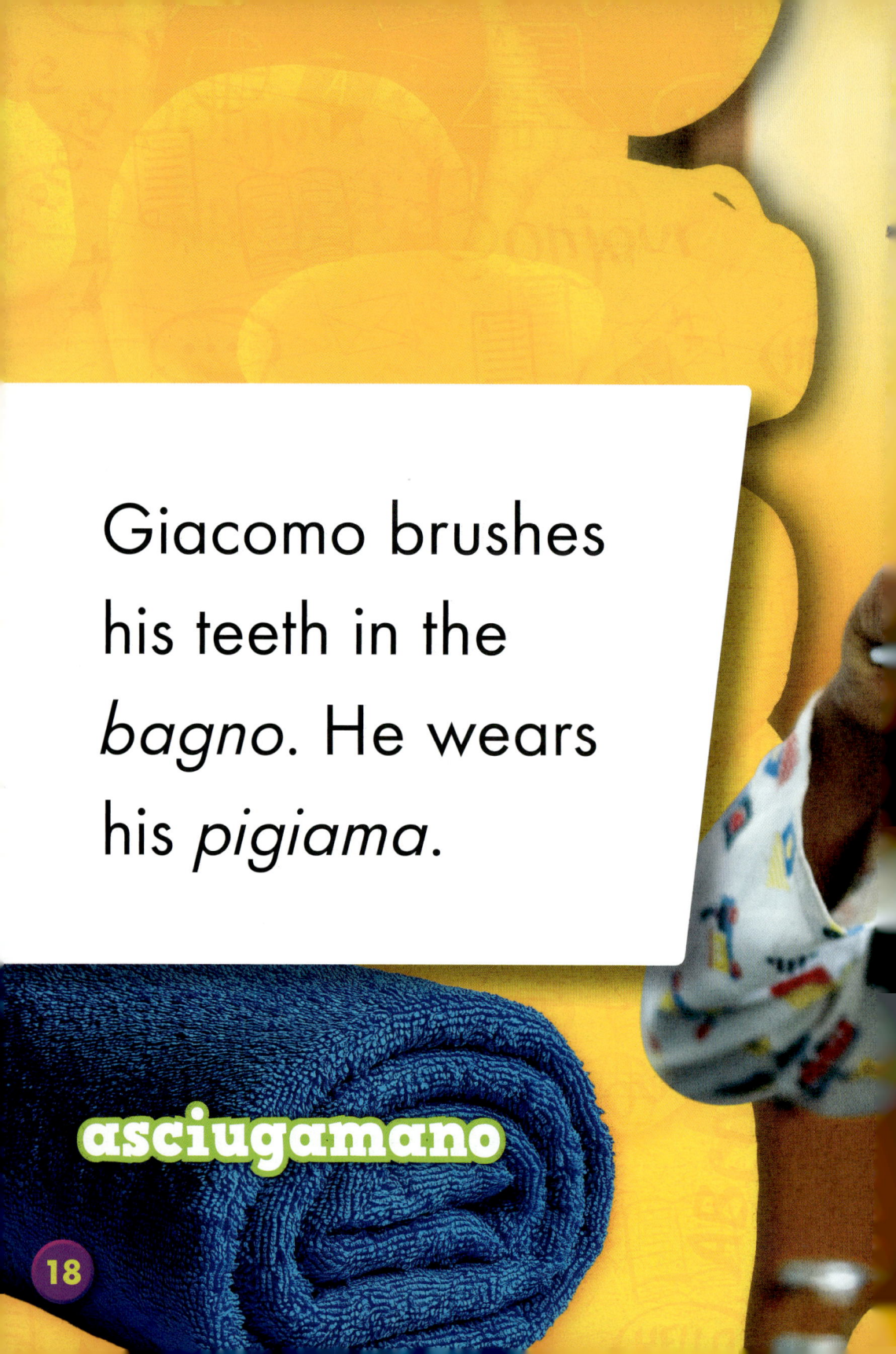

Giacomo brushes his teeth in the *bagno*. He wears his *pigiama*.

asciugamano

18

pigiama

Words to Know

- bagno (BAHN-yoh) .... bathroom
- asciugamano (ah-SHU-gah-MAH-noh).....
.... towel
- lavandino (lah-vahn-DEE-noh) .... sink
- pigiama (pee-JAHM-ah) .... pajamas

Buonanotte!

The *gatto* is asleep
on Alice's *letto*.
She is sleepy, too.
Buonanotte!

buonanotte
(BWO-nah-NOH-tay)
good night

gatto

Words to Know

- gatto (GAHT-toh)...................................cat
- letto (LEH-toh)....................................bed
- lampada (LAHM-pah-dah)...............lamp
- coperta (coh-PEHR-tah)..............blanket
- arrivederci (ah-REE-vah-DER-chee).......
  ....goodbye

21

Glossary

gelato

a soft, rich Italian ice cream

pasta al pomodoro

a pasta dish with a fresh tomato sauce

passeggiata

a slow walk, often in the evening

piazza

a public city or town square

To Learn More

AT THE LIBRARY

Booth, Thomas. *Italian English Illustrated Dictionary*. New York, N.Y.: DK Publishing, 2023.

Gleisner, Jenna Lee. *My First Look at Italian*. Minneapolis, Minn.: Jump!, 2020.

Sabelko, Rebecca. *Italy*. Minneapolis, Minn.: Bellwether Media, 2023.

ON THE WEB

FACTSURFER

Factsurfer.com gives you a safe, fun way to find more information.

1. Go to www.factsurfer.com.

2. Enter "Italian" into the search box and click 🔍.

3. Select your book cover to see a list of related content.

Index

The images in this book are reproduced through the courtesy of: Lorado/ Getty Images, front cover; King, p. 3; N Lawrenson/ peopleimages.com, pp. 4-5; travnikovstudio, pp. 6-7; Tu.kc, p. 8 (pesce); StockImageFactory.com, pp. 8-9; Iryna, p. 10 (tazza); Arianne, pp. 10-11; david_franklin, p. 12 (forbici); shironosov, pp. 12-13; ChiccoDodiFC, pp. 14-15; André Polvani, p. 16 (gelato); Moyo Studio/ Getty Images, pp. 16-17; MS, p. 18 (asciugamano); FG Trade, pp. 18-19; Leonid Ikan, pp. 20-21; EdNurg, p. 22 (gelato); Steve Lovegrove, p. 22 (passeggiata); Alessio Orrù, p. 22 (pasta al pomodoro); Nicola Forenza, p. 22 (piazza).